AF380754

# better together*

*This book is best read together, grownup and kid.

**akidsco.com**

a
kids
book
about

# a kids book about about BOUNDARIES

**by Ashley Bendiksen**

**A Kids Book About**
**Editor** Emma Wolf
**Head of Design** Rick DeLucco
**Publisher** Jelani Memory

**DK**
**Senior Production Editor** Jennifer Murray
**Senior Production Controller** Louise Minihane
**Managing Editor** Hazel Eriksson
**Publishing Director** Mark Searle

This American Edition, 2026
Published in the United States by DK Publishing,
a Division of Penguin Random House LLC
1745 Broadway, 20th Floor, New York, NY 10019





First published in Great Britain in 2026 by
Dorling Kindersley Limited, 20 Vauxhall Bridge Road, London SW1V 2SA
A Penguin Random House Company

The authorised representative in the EEA is
Dorling Kindersley Verlag GmbH. Arnulfstr. 124, 80636 Munich, Germany

A CIP catalogue record for this book is available from the British Library

ISBN 978-0-2417-8605-5

DK books are available at special discounts when purchased in bulk for
sales promotions, premiums, fund-raising, or educational use. For details, contact:
DK Publishing Special Markets, 1745 Broadway, 20th Floor, New York, NY 10019, or
SpecialSales@dk.com

Printed and bound in China

**www.dk.com**

**akidsco.com**


**Interested in bringing Ashley Bendiksen to your school or event?**
**Visit topyouthspeakers.com/ashley**

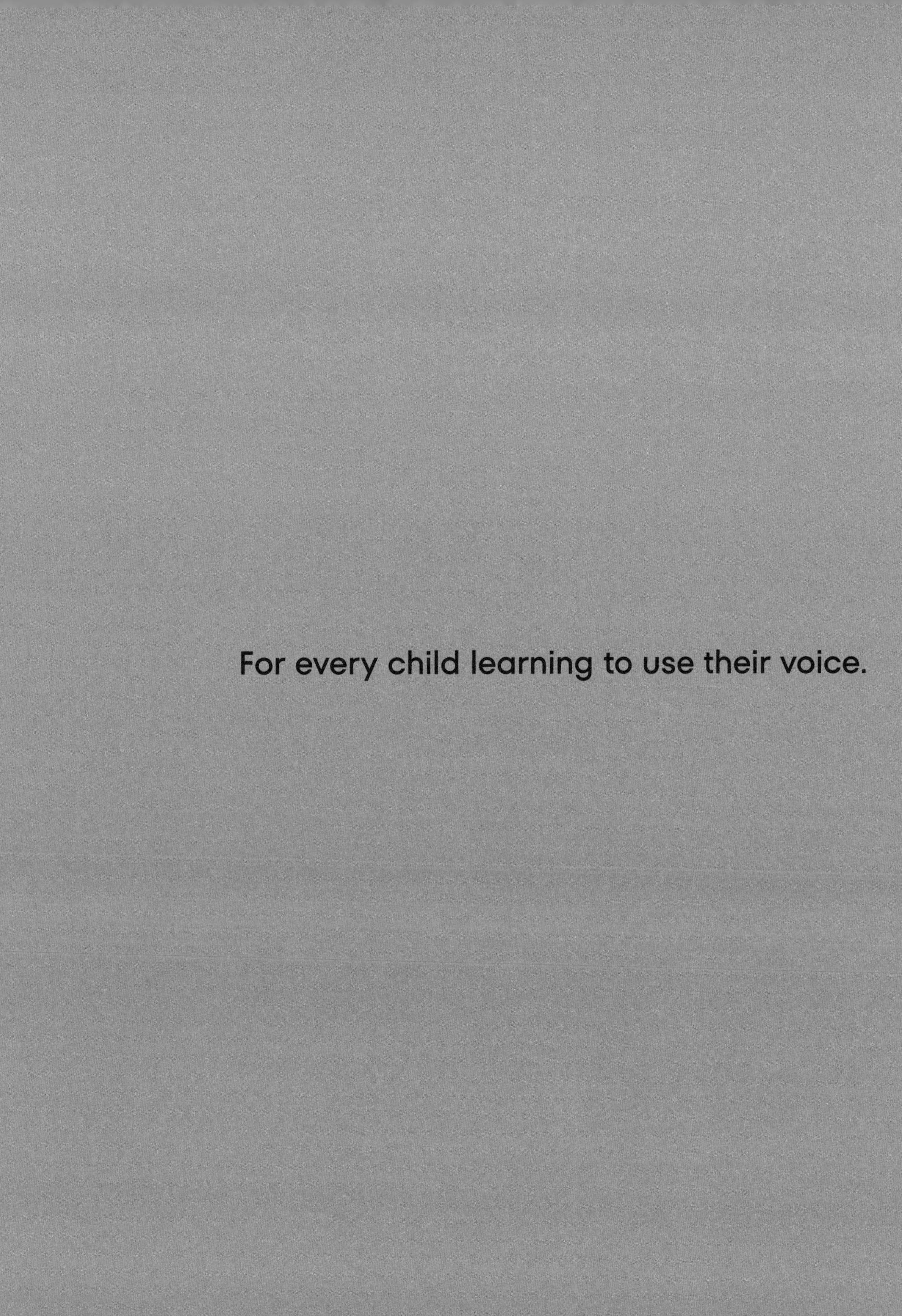

For every child learning to use their voice.

# Intro
## for grownups

**R**elationships are a really big part of our lives. Most people have lots of them! There's family members—like parents, siblings, grandparents, aunts, uncles, and cousins. And people outside your family—like friends, neighbors, teachers, and classmates. As you grow up, you'll build even more relationships! That's just part of being human.

To live a happy and safe life, it's important to make sure these relationships are healthy. How do you do that? You use your voice to set boundaries. "Bounda-what?" Don't worry, this book will explain everything!

What matters most is knowing that you have the power to speak up about how people treat you. And you should! I mean, no one's a mind reader—that'd be kinda weird!

This book will show you a skill you can start using today, and keep using for the rest of your life. Pretty cool, right? I'm so glad you're reading this. Let's get started!

When I was little, I was a 

CONFIDENT, AND OUTGOING KID.

I liked

SCHOOL, DANCING, AND PLAYING WITH MY LITTLE SISTERS!

Then one day, things changed.

I FELT SAD AND UNSAFE
A LOT OF THE TIME.

It wasn't because there were
monsters hiding under my bed,
or a big earthquake on the way.

It was because people
in my life made me feel bad.

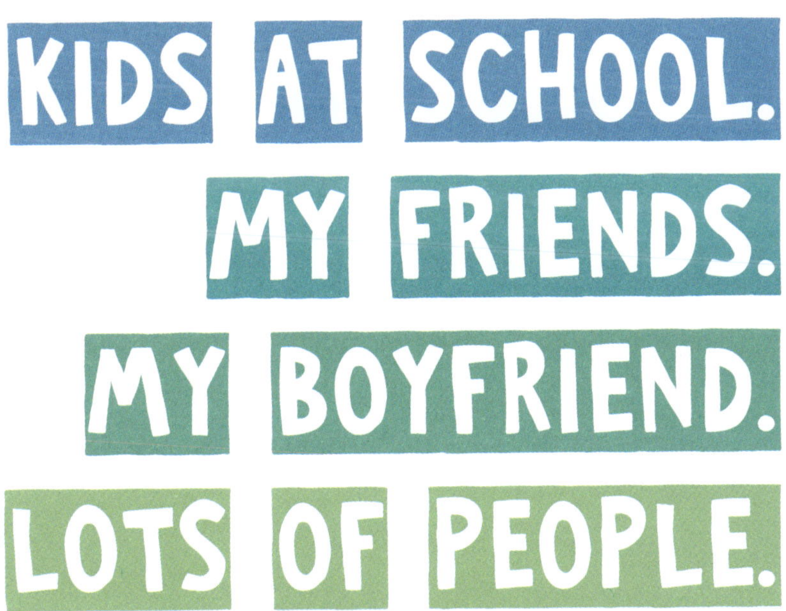

To make it better,
I tried to ignore
the things they said
or wanted me to do.

BUT THAT DIDN'T WORK.

What worked was learning how to

# SPEAK

UP.

I'm Ashley, and I help kids like you feel safe and happy by setting

# BOUNDARIES.

Have you heard this word before?

If this is a new idea for you,
know it was new for me, too!

You see, sometimes in life,
people can make us feel
bad about ourselves.

SOMETIMES, PEOPLE ARE HURTFUL ON PURPOSE.

SOMETIMES, PEOPLE ARE HURTFUL BY ACCIDENT.

SOMETIMES, PEOPLE AND THINGS JUST MAKE US FEEL UNCOMFORTABLE.

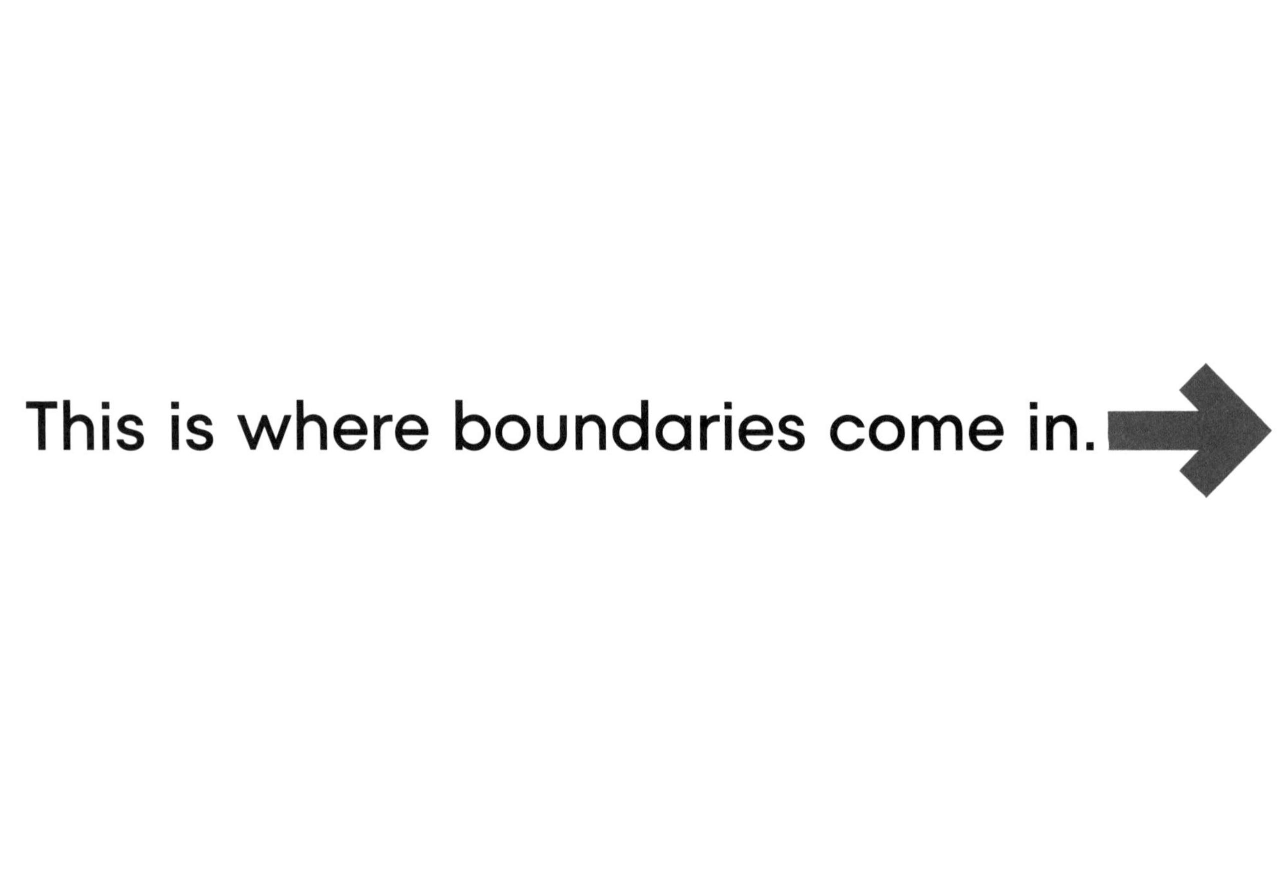

This is where boundaries come in.

# BOUNDARIES

are how we tell others what is **OK** with us...and what is not **OK**.

# BOUNDARIES

protect our bodies and our feelings.

THEY'RE HOW WE KEEP OURSELVES SAFE.

For example, as a kid,
I was afraid of dogs.

Even though I didn't
want to be near them,
grownups always made me.

I felt like my feelings
didn't matter.

And like I didn't
have a voice.

Then, as I grew up,
this happened even more.

I felt pressured to do
what other people wanted,
even when it didn't feel right.

AND THIS LEFT ME

HURT.

But I'm here to tell you
that we **all** have a voice.

And it's a

POWER

# FUL VOICE.

You can speak up
if something feels uncomfortable
or doesn't feel right for you.

Making sense so far?

Let's think about it like this...

Imagine you live on
your own little planet.

And on this planet, you get to
make the rules for how things work:

WHO'S ALLOWED TO VISIT.

HOW PEOPLE BEHAVE.

WHAT KEEPS YOUR
PLANET HEALTHY.

If someone doesn't follow the rules,
they won't be allowed on your planet.

It's the exact same for you
and your life on *this* planet.

You get to choose
what is best for you.

# YES, YOU ACTUALLY DO.

Your body and your
feelings belong to you.

You have a right to feel
safe and respected.

You get to decide what
keeps you healthy.

AND IT'S SO IMPOR

TANT THAT YOU DO.

Let's take a closer look
at how boundaries work.

There are two big types
of boundaries:

PHYSICAL

AND

EMOTIONAL.

# PHYSICAL BOUNDARIES

protect things like your body, belongings, and personal space.

This might be how someone touches you, or when they can play with your toys.

# EMOTIONAL BOUNDARIES

protect things like
your feelings and emotions.

This might be how people talk
to you, or the jokes they tell.

Whenever something doesn't
feel OK, you can use your voice
and set a boundary!

*Here are some ways
you might do this:*

Say,

when you don't want to
give someone a hug.

Say,



when a game stops feeling fun.

Say,



when someone is trying
to get you to break a rule.

You can also make a request:

Say,
**"LET'S DO THIS INSTEAD,"**
when you want to play
a different game.

Say,
**"PLEASE ASK ME
FIRST NEXT TIME,"**
when someone uses your
things without asking.

Say,
**"I NEED SOME TIME
TO THINK ABOUT THAT,"**
when you're not sure
what to say or do yet.

# BOUNDARIES GIVE YOU

# POWER.

Especially when you feel
like you don't have power.

But here's the thing—
not everyone will listen to
or respect your boundaries.

So, what do you do then?

You can:

WALK AWAY FROM A SITUATION.
ASK TO STOP SPENDING TIME WITH SOMEONE.
TALK TO A TRUSTED GROWNUP.

Because remember,

# TO DECIDE

what's best for you.

Still, it's not always
easy to set boundaries.

## SOMETIMES,

you have to say no—
even to people you love.

# SOMETIMES,

you'll change your mind,
or have different boundaries
with different people.

It's really important
to take care of yourself first.

And as much as
your boundaries matter...

# SO DO EVERYONE ELSE'S.

Just like you,
other people have
boundaries, too.

It's important for people
to respect your boundaries
and for you to respect theirs.

Because

# EVER

# YONE

deserves to feel respected and safe!

One of the best ways
to do this is to always ASK first:

CAN I PLAY WITH YOUR TOY?

CAN I GIVE YOU A HUG?

CAN I COME OVER TO YOUR HOUSE?

If they say, "NO,"

just say,

"OK, NO PROBLEM!"

Because when you do,
you'll make them feel safe.

And when everyone's boundaries
are honored, we all become
happier and safer.

Today, I have awesome people
in my life (and I love dogs now!)

I feel safe and supported.

I use my voice and set boundaries.

And now, you can, too.

YOU MATTER...
AND SO DOES

YOUR VOICE.

# Outro
## for grownups

**Y**ou did it!! I already knew you were smart... but now you're a seriously smart kid for knowing about boundaries. A lot of kids—and even grownups—don't know this. But you do!

So, what's next? Ask a grownup any questions you might have. Start using your new skill. Has anyone ever made you feel uncomfortable? If you could travel back in time, what boundary would you set? Does anyone make you feel uncomfortable now?

From this day forward, if someone's behavior bothers you, ask yourself, "How can I set a boundary?" If you need ideas about what to do, talk to a safe, trusted grownup. You can always re-read this book, too!

If I could time travel, I'd set lots of boundaries. I just wish I knew what you know now!

I'm so proud of you for learning this. Keep using your voice. You've got this.

*A note to grownups: Teaching boundaries is all about balance. It's important to teach kids kindness and affection—but even more important to include their voice. Talk about this together, and let them know that their comfort matters.*

# About The Author

Ashley Bendiksen (she/her) has dedicated her life's work to empowering people impacted by adversity—especially youth. A nationally recognized speaker and expert in abuse prevention and trauma resilience, she travels the US speaking to students and educators about healthy relationships, self-advocacy, ACEs (Adverse Childhood Experiences), and trauma-informed care. A survivor herself, Ashley turned hardship into purpose. Despite becoming homeless and a college dropout, she graduated as Valedictorian, became an activist, and built a career in advocacy, prevention, and policy change. This is the book Ashley needed as a kid—a reminder that even when we feel powerless, we still have power.

When she isn't speaking, Ashley lives by the ocean in Rhode Island, where she loves biking, hiking, journaling, and playing piano.

 @ashleybendiksen      @myafterstory      ashleybendiksen.com

# Made to empower.

# Discover more at akidsco.com